Happy 1st Mother's Day to
Lily and Jen with love
from Papa Skip 5/14/06

A New Frog

My First Look At

The Life Cycle of an Amphibian

Written by Pamela Hickman
Illustrated by Heather Collins

Kids Can Press

This is the pond

that Jenny explores.

This is the frog

that sings in the pond

that Jenny explores.

This is the mate
that joined the frog,
that sings in the pond
that Jenny explores.

These are the eggs
that were laid by the mate,
that joined the frog,
that sings in the pond
that Jenny explores.

These are the tadpoles
that hatched from the eggs,
that were laid by the mate,
that joined the frog,
that sings in the pond
that Jenny explores.

These are the froglets
that grew from the tadpoles,
that hatched from the eggs,
that were laid by the mate,
that joined the frog,
that sings in the pond
that Jenny explores.

These are the new frogs

that grew from the froglets,

that grew from the tadpoles,

that hatched from the eggs,

that were laid by the mate,

that joined the frog,

that sings in the pond

that Jenny explores.

Watch out!

Note to Parents

You have just seen the life cycle of a Leopard Frog. Like most amphibians, frogs mate, lay their eggs and develop into adults in the water. The Leopard Frog completes its life cycle in one summer, but some frogs, such as Bullfrogs, take up to two years to change and grow into adults.

Visit a pond with your family and explore the water for tadpoles and other small creatures. Here are two easy ways to get a closer look at a pond's amazing aquatic life: (1) Dip a small net or kitchen strainer into the pond near the shoreline plants and empty it into a large glass jar or a basin filled with pond water. If you look closely, you'll see some of the pond creatures illustrated in this book, and you'll probably find lots more. When you've finished watching the creatures, return them to the pond. (2) To make a waterscope similar to the one Jenny uses to look at the frog spawn, you'll need an empty juice can with both ends removed. Stretch a piece of plastic wrap over one end. Secure it with an elastic band and then with waterproof tape. Put the covered end in the water, and peer through the open end to see what's swimming below the surface.

Explore the same pond with your family several times throughout the year to see how the plants and animals change. Each visit will bring a new discovery.

For Jenny — P.H.
For Tara — H.C.

Text copyright © 1999 by Pamela Hickman
Illustrations copyright © 1999 by Heather Collins/Glyphics

Kids Can Press acknowledges the financial support of the Ontario Arts
Council, the Canada Council for the Arts and the Government of Canada,
through the BPIDP, for our publishing activity.

Published in Canada by
Kids Can Press Ltd.
29 Birch Avenue
Toronto, ON M4V 1E2

Published in the U.S. by
Kids Can Press Ltd.
4500 Witmer Estates
Niagara Falls, NY 14305-1386

The artwork in this book was rendered in watercolor and gouache.

Edited by Linda Biesenthal
Designed by Blair Kerrigan/Glyphics
Printed in Hong Kong by Wing King Tong Co. Ltd.

CM 99 0 9 8 7 6 5 4 3 2

Canadian Cataloguing in Publication Data

Hickman, Pamela
      A new frog : my first look at the life cycle of an amphibian

ISBN 1-55074-615-4

1. Frogs — Life cycles — Juvenile literature. I. Collins, Heather. II. Title.

QL668.E2H52 1999   j571.8'1789   C98-932263-7

Kids Can Press is a Nelvana company